The Nature Conservancy of Canada is proud to present you with this story of our conservation work in the Squamish/Brackendale region of British Columbia, benefiting bald eagles, salmon populations, working forests and the community.

Our ongoing project seeks to blend environmental protection with economic stability in the Squamish Valley and encompasses the interests of many groups and individuals who have assisted our work. We thank them for their support, and most particularly acknowledge the Forest Alliance of British Columbia, without whose generous leadership contribution, protection of this unique natural heritage would not be possible.

*Elva Kyle*
Vice Chair
Board of Trustees

BEAUTIFUL
BRITISH COLUMBIA

# The Book of Eagles

IMAGES B.C./IMAGE NETWORK

NATURE
CONSERVANCY
CANADA

BEAUTIFUL
BRITISH COLUMBIA
*Magazine*

BEAUTIFUL
BRITISH COLUMBIA
*Magazine*

Published by
Beautiful British Columbia Magazine
A Division of Great Pacific Industries Inc.
in association with
The Nature Conservancy of Canada

To order copies of this book in Canada or the USA
call 1–800–663–7611 or fax 1–800–308–4533
To order copies of this book worldwide
call (604)384–5456 or fax (604)384–2812

Beautiful British Columbia
929 Ellery Street
Victoria, British Columbia
Canada V9A 7B4

Canadian Cataloguing in Publication Data
Main entry under title: The book of eagles
ISBN 0-920431-31-3
1. Eagles. 2. Eagles—Pictorial works.
I. McCartie, Gary, 1941–.
II. The Nature Conservancy of Canada.
III. Beautiful British Columbia Magazine (Firm)
QL696.F32B66 1995     598.9'16     C95-911146-8

Printed in Canada

# Foreword

This book is about and for the eagles of Brackendale. No one is sure how long these bald eagles have been wintering in the area near this village on the lower reaches of the Squamish River in southwestern British Columbia. What is known is that the numbers of this magnificent white-headed raptor have grown so great that the village and the Squamish Valley may now host the single largest winter habitat of bald eagles in the world.

This gathering of eagles, however, is at risk from human encroachment. Losing this safe winter home after having lost so many others would be a severe blow with dire consequences for bald eagles everywhere.

People who understand the importance of protecting the habitat of "the kings of birds and birds of kings" are coming together to take action, in Brackendale and the Squamish Valley, in British Columbia and across Canada.

This book, conceived by The Nature Conservancy of Canada, is but one way of taking action. It aims to make more people aware of what is at stake for the eagles — and what losing them would mean. All profits from the sale of The Book of Eagles will go to help protect eagle habitat in the Squamish Valley in perpetuity.

People and organizations throughout the province are lending support in many ways. This book is being published at no charge by a B.C. publisher, Beautiful British Columbia, and major financial support for the entire project of protecting eagle habitat is being provided by the Forest Alliance of British Columbia. Others who are donating goods, services, time and energy are listed on pages 62 and 63.

On behalf of the eagles of Brackendale, the creators of this book thank everyone who is helping to safeguard their future.

FRANK OBERLE

# Rhythm of

# the Land

# Rhythm of the Land

They say every picture tells a story. To see a bald eagle perching in a majestic black cottonwood in the broad Squamish Valley beneath a snowcapped volcanic mountain is to tell a story of dazzling complexity, profound simplicity and, ultimately, hope.

The eagles of Brackendale's story began when the world was young. It is intimately linked with one of nature's oldest movements — the steady drifting of enormous "plates" of the earth's crust. This ceaseless sliding has existed for hundreds of millions of years — silent, relentless and so powerful it transforms the face of the planet. Embedded in many of these tectonic plates are the continents, which the plates carry around the globe in an unpredictable choreography. Unimaginably slow, each step in this geological dance takes millions of years.

The dance, seldom smooth, is especially jarring where plates meet. Continent-carrying plates can collide with such force they thrust up whole mountain ranges, such as the Himalayas. An ocean plate slipping under a continental plate can also throw mountains, such as the Rockies, miles above the surface. And sometimes plates slide past each other, shearing off edges in sudden spasms along fault lines. All the boundary lines between these moving plates are hot spots for earthquakes and volcanic eruptions.

The west coast of Canada lies along the fault line marking the meeting of the Pacific Ocean and North American plates. Like the rest of the west coast from Alaska to Chile, it is strung with chains of mountains and perforated with volcanoes. Multiple mountain ranges crease the province's mainland coast with hundreds of dramatic fiords. The Squamish Valley and Howe Sound in southwestern British Columbia are two of these sculpted marvels.

This geologic work of art owes part of its glory to glaciation, one of nature's cycles measured not in millions of years, as are the movements of continents, but in tens of thousands of years. About 60,000 years ago, the Earth's atmosphere began to slowly cool. Snow stayed year round on the higher peaks and glaciers grew. And grew. Like the proverbial snowball down the side of the hill, the glaciers expanded relentlessly as they crept down and filled the valleys. In time they became a massive sheet of ice, covering much of Canada.

CAMERON HERYET/IMAGE NETWORK

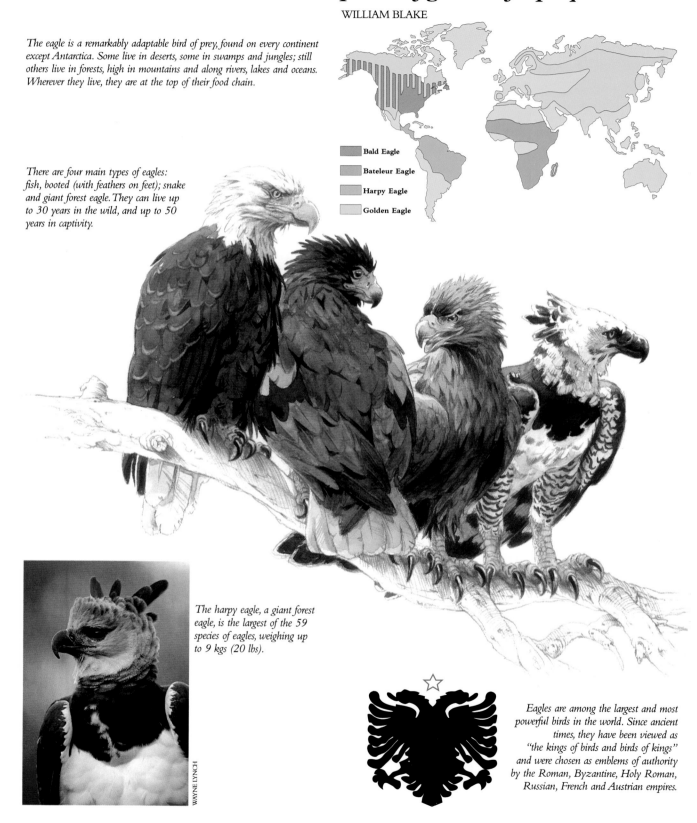

> ## *"When thou seest an eagle, thou seest a portion of genius. Lift up thy head."*
> WILLIAM BLAKE

*The eagle is a remarkably adaptable bird of prey, found on every continent except Antarctica. Some live in deserts, some in swamps and jungles; still others live in forests, high in mountains and along rivers, lakes and oceans. Wherever they live, they are at the top of their food chain.*

■ Bald Eagle
■ Bateleur Eagle
■ Harpy Eagle
■ Golden Eagle

*There are four main types of eagles: fish, booted (with feathers on feet); snake and giant forest eagle. They can live up to 30 years in the wild, and up to 50 years in captivity.*

*The harpy eagle, a giant forest eagle, is the largest of the 59 species of eagles, weighing up to 9 kgs (20 lbs).*

WAYNE LYNCH

*Eagles are among the largest and most powerful birds in the world. Since ancient times, they have been viewed as "the kings of birds and birds of kings" and were chosen as emblems of authority by the Roman, Byzantine, Holy Roman, Russian, French and Austrian empires.*

Three periods of warming chased back the ice, which only returned to fill the valleys. In each of these cycles lasting thousands of years, ice rivers inched their way through the valleys. The sheer weight of the ice pack ground the mountain rock beneath it. Massive scouring pads of solid ice scraped off stones of every size and shape, which in turn became tools for carving steep slopes and flattening valley floors. Boulders and pebbles were carried away to be left where they sat when the next warming reversed the ice flow.

The last of these three glaciations peaked about 14,000 years ago. The ice pack, up to 1,524 metres (5,000 feet) deep, filled the Squamish Valley and stretched as far south as Seattle. An eagle surveying the Antarctic-like wasteland would see a vast sea of ice, dotted with islands that were really the tips of the tallest mountains. Then about 10,000 years ago, what is now called Mount Garibaldi erupted in a fiery volcanic display. Streams of lava seared glacial ice, which melted into mountain lakes.

At about the same time as the eruption, the glaciers began receding for the third and last time. On the valley floors, they left massive moraines — enormous piles of rock rubble they had scraped from distant mountain sides. Rivers roared through freshly carved valleys, swollen with melting glacial water. They carried ton upon ton of silt and mineral debris that would serve as raw material for the rich soil of the temperate rainforest — and rock that would become the gravel beds of rich salmon spawning grounds.

FRANK OBERLE

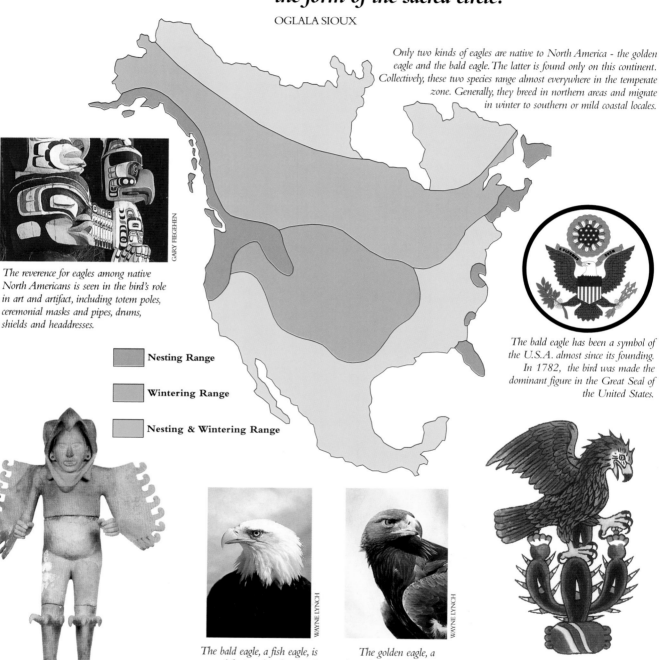

*"The eagle is the chief of birds because it flies higher, sees all and moves through the sky in the form of the sacred circle."*

OGLALA SIOUX

Only two kinds of eagles are native to North America - the golden eagle and the bald eagle. The latter is found only on this continent. Collectively, these two species range almost everywhere in the temperate zone. Generally, they breed in northern areas and migrate in winter to southern or mild coastal locales.

The reverence for eagles among native North Americans is seen in the bird's role in art and artifact, including totem poles, ceremonial masks and pipes, drums, shields and headdresses.

**Nesting Range**

**Wintering Range**

**Nesting & Wintering Range**

The bald eagle has been a symbol of the U.S.A. almost since its founding. In 1782, the bird was made the dominant figure in the Great Seal of the United States.

This Aztec sculpture represents an eagle warrior, one of the two most prestigious military orders of the Aztecs; the other was the jaguar.

The bald eagle, a fish eagle, is named for its white head and tail feathers. "Balled" is a Middle English word for white. Bald eagles thrive wherever there is a large body of water, big trees and a plentiful supply of fish.

The golden eagle, a booted eagle, is named for its gold head feathers. It prefers remote mountain and high plains habitats and hunts small game.

In Aztec legend, the god Huitzilopochtli told his people to build a city where they saw an eagle eating a snake while sitting on a cactus. Tenochitlan, the settlement the Aztecs founded where they saw such a scene, is today the site of Mexico City.

Released from the enormous pressure of the glacial ice, the unburdened land rose by up to 100 metres in some places. Yet the rapid melting also caused sea levels to rise so high it submerged some of this newly elevated land. The border where land met sea swayed back and forth. This helped form fertile ground for what would become the rich Squamish estuary.

Farther up the valley, however, hardy lichens took hold on rock, and in time contributed to the formation of soils which could sustain more advanced plants. Bit by bit the world warmed, the land became more fertile and within a few centuries this tundra became blanketed by pine and spruce. As the climate and environment changed, animal life established itself. Birds, sustained by insects, migrated north. Small rodents followed them as vegetation continued to flourish, and in time there came deer, elk, moose, wolf, grizzly and cougar. It is certain that eagles watched all this unfold.

The forest continued to evolve, nurtured by moisture-laden ocean winds, dry summers and rich soils of the valley floor. Giant spruce, western red cedar, hemlock and Douglas fir emerged in the continuous cycle of species' rise to dominance.

Finally, about 5,000 years ago, the level of the Pacific Ocean settled and the delta of the Squamish Valley began to appear as it does today, threaded by five glacial rivers that meet in the Squamish floodplain: the Squamish, Elaho, Ashlu, Cheakamus and Mamquam. The rivers continued to shape and nourish the flatland with annual deposits. And each year the rich forest lands and salt marsh moved a bit farther south.

With the passing of this last glacial period and tidal zone stability, another of nature's rhythms returned, one measured by single years rather than thousands: it was the annual return of salmon up the rivers to spawn, and die in beds where they had started life's journey.

AL HARVEY

*"He clasps the crag with crooked hands,*
*Close to the sun in lonely lands,*
*Ringed with the azure world he stands,*
*The wrinkled sea beneath him crawls,*
*He watches from his mountain walls;*
*And, like a thunderbolt, he falls."*

from "The Eagle" by ALFRED LORD TENNYSON

### The Bald Eagle Family Tree

| | |
|---|---|
| *Class: Aves* | *Vital Statistics* |
| *Order: Falconiformes* | *Size:* 75-100 cm; (30-40 in) |
| *Family: Accipitridae* | *Wingspan:* 180-230 cm (6-7.5 ft) |
| *Genus: Haliaeetus* | *Weight:* Female, 3.5-5.6 kg (8-12 lbs) |
| *Species: Haliaeetus leucocephalus* | Male, 3.5-4 kg (8-9 lbs) |

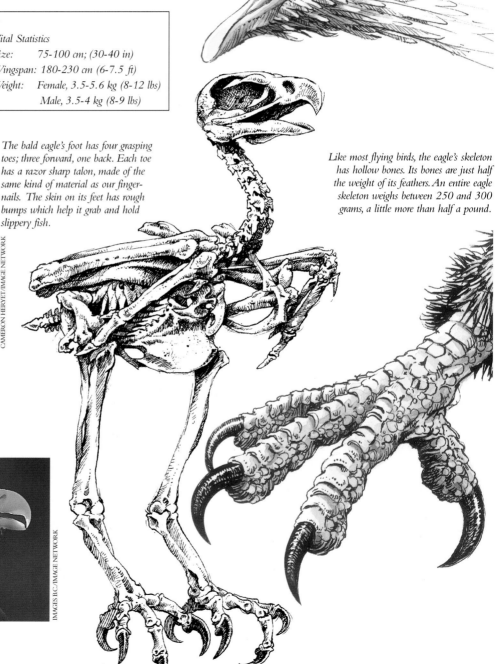

*The bald eagle's foot has four grasping toes; three forward, one back. Each toe has a razor sharp talon, made of the same kind of material as our fingernails. The skin on its feet has rough bumps which help it grab and hold slippery fish.*

CAMERON HERYET/IMAGE NETWORK

*Like most flying birds, the eagle's skeleton has hollow bones. Its bones are just half the weight of its feathers. An entire eagle skeleton weighs between 250 and 300 grams, a little more than half a pound.*

*The bald eagle's beak is hooked for tearing meat. Powerful jaw muscles give it great biting strength, and the beak constantly sharpens itself through use. Just above the beak is the cere, a patch of bare skin that has two nostrils.*

IMAGES B.C./IMAGE NETWORK

There had not been an established Squamish River system for thousands of years. Yet the salmon had the ability to survive during the advance and retreat of glaciers to continue their life cycle. They were able to find and colonize suitable new streams fed by melting glaciers, and their eggs were perfectly suited to winter in these pristine young streams.

These waters and river beds lacked the ability to nourish newly hatched salmon, but the eggs contained enough food for the developing embryos to survive until their parents' own bodies had decayed. This provided the river with the nutrients needed to sustain the lives of the next generation. The salmon, in effect, bring nutrients to the river from the sea in the form of their bodies which grow to adulthood in the ocean.

Ever since the glaciers' last retreat, the salmon have been returning to — and "fertilizing" — the gravel spawning beds throughout the Squamish Valley.

The salmon cycle of death and rebirth is intimately linked to still more rhythmic patterns. The return and spawning are exquisitely timed to the arrival of the autumnal rains of the temperate rainforest. And the hatching in spring follows in step with the sun's return to spark the bloom of algae and floodplain forest growth, which are both nourished by the rotting salmon carcasses. The algae and new leaves feed micro-organisms and insects, which in turn nourish the young salmon. And so the cycle continues, a rhythm within the larger rhythm of glaciation and the dance of continents.

FRANK OBERLE

# A Gathering

# of Eagles

# A Gathering of Eagles

The annual return of spawning salmon to the Squamish River watershed makes possible another step in the dance of life — the arrival of migratory bald eagles for the winter season. The watershed, with its numerous valleys, rivers, channels and sandbars, large and small creeks, fragile marshes and evergreen forest, is a kind of paradise for eagles. The watershed has supported a resident population of bald eagles since the last retreat of the glaciers. It has also supported an overwintering population. Here they find the large old trees they prefer for roosting and perching, a mild sea-tempered climate, and most important for migratory birds in the winter months, a plentiful food supply in the carcasses of spawned-out salmon. The fish, in fact, provide one of the most abundant winter feasts in North America.

Today six species of salmon return to the Squamish watershed. Pink, also called humpback salmon, sockeye and chinook return in the fall. Coho, steelhead and chum, also called dog salmon, return in winter. Chum are particularly abundant. They prefer the relatively slow water of the lower reaches of the Squamish system — the second largest salmon river in southwestern British Columbia after the Fraser.

Chinook, coho, sockeye and steelhead salmon stocks in the Squamish system have been dramatically depleted. Pink salmon are on the rebound, and chum, the most rugged salmon, continues to have the highest return rate. Much of the chum's strong showing is due to habitat enhancement in the Squamish watershed. One estimate is that the watershed's rivers now support from 150,000 to 450,000 chum salmon. Their death is the signal for the eagles to start gathering.

It is thought that eagles come from as far east as Wisconsin, as far south as Arizona and as far north as Alaska, but most come from B.C.'s northern Interior and north coast. In the autumn months, they ride thermals and updrafts, follow ridges and mountainsides leading down to the southwest coast. Though powerful, skillful fliers, these birds conserve energy by gliding as much as possible. Riding the winds, they can achieve speeds of up to 80 kilometres per hour (50 mph) and travel up to 300 kilometres (180 miles) in a single flight.

CAMERON HERYET/IMAGE NETWORK

## "A lover's eyes will gaze an eagle blind."

from Love's Labour's Lost, by WILLIAM SHAKESPEARE

CAMERON HERVEY/IMAGE NETWORK

Eagle eyes face forward like human eyes. This gives them binocular, three-dimensional vision, which enables them to judge distance and speed. Eagle vision is so acute that experts believe they can see a rabbit from three kilometres (two miles). That's almost eight times sharper than a person with 20/20 vision.

Eagles also have two foveae, or centres of focus, enabling them to focus both forward and sideways. A special transparent eyelid, known as the nictitating membrane, slides across the eye, protecting it from dust and danger, while still allowing the eagle to see.

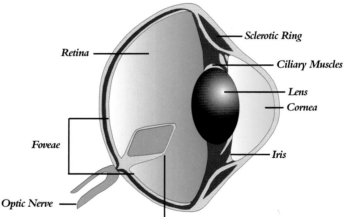

Retina

Sclerotic Ring

Ciliary Muscles

Lens

Cornea

Iris

Foveae

Optic Nerve

Pecten

BOB HERGER

Right behind an eagle's eyes are its ears, hidden from view under a layer of special feathers. Among the most social of all birds of prey, bald eagles are very vocal birds.

In Greek mythology, Aquila was the bird of Zeus, king of the gods. Zeus asked Aquila to use its eagle eye to find the world's most beautiful youth. The eagle snatched up the Trojan boy Ganymede and took him to Olympus to become cupbearer to the gods. Zeus was so pleased, he rewarded Aquila a place in the sky - the constellation that bears its name.

AQUILA

Precisely how these eagles find a particular winter habitat remains a mystery. Some scientists believe it is based on past experience. Others think the explanation lies in their remarkable eyesight and flying abilities. The bird's habit of flying high may enable them to see concentrations of other eagles up to 30 kilometres (18 miles) away. A concentration of fellow eagles is a sure sign of an ample food supply. And so a gathering begins.

By day the eagles forage by stream banks. When not feasting on salmon carcasses on the ground, they perch in deciduous and coniferous trees close to feeding areas. There they preen their feathers, sleep and generally conserve energy.

Eagles have been seen roosting throughout the Squamish Valley, in both lowland deciduous and upland coniferous forests. These roost sites can take the form of individual cottonwood trees, large cottonwood groves, or large patches of old-growth coniferous forest. Some of these ancient conifers may have been

seedlings when Norman invaders fought Anglo-Saxons at the Battle of Hastings and labourers fitted together stones to complete the Great Wall of China.

In their winter habitat, bald eagles congregate, sometimes up to a dozen birds per branch. No one is certain why wintering bald eagles gather this way. Some scientists believe eagles cluster for security, since they often sleep for long periods. Clustering may also allow younger eagles to learn social and hunting skills.

Bald eagles eat voraciously in winter. Each bird needs to eat up to 1/10th of its body weight every day. To survive the winter they need an abundant food supply, one that doesn't demand a great deal of energy to find and kill. This is particularly true for still-maturing juveniles who have neither the skills nor seniority to harvest available prey. The salmon feast of the Squamish is just such a food supply.

It is not, however, all take and no give. The bald eagles actually help the salmon cycle complete itself. In tearing apart the carcasses with their powerful

GRAHAM OSBORNE

# "Houston, Tranquility Base here. The Eagle has landed."

NEIL ARMSTRONG, July 20, 1969

The Archaeopteryx, or "ancient wing," is believed to have been the earliest bird, living about 130 million years ago. The flight feathers on this half-bird, half-reptile looked much like those of birds today.

THOMAS KITCHEN/FIRST LIGHT

Flight feathers - primary, secondary and tertiary - are found on wings and tail. Down feathers keep birds warm, and contour feathers give a bird its shape. Moulting in eagles is believed to occur mostly in summer, but does not involve all feathers at once.

FRANK OBERLE

KHAREN HILL

Eagles have about 7,000 feathers, but all together they weigh just over half a kilogram, or a little more than a pound. A feather's intricate, interlocking structure is comprised of shafts, barbs, barbules and barbicels. These elements form a smooth, flat web that protects the birds from water and wind. Eagles preen their feathers using oil from the uriphygeal gland at the base of their tails.

A typical wing feather arrangement has tertiaries growing closest to the body, followed by the secondaries and the long, stiff primaries.

In many native North American cultures, a person may not tell a lie when holding an eagle feather, just as in Christian cultures court witnesses place their hand on a Bible and swear to tell the truth.

beaks, the eagles fertilize the river with the bits and pieces of remaining carcass that are left in and by the river. These remains serve as fertilizer for the algae and streamside plants that bloom in spring. Insects eat the algae and other plants. Young salmon eat the insects and grow to complete their role in the endlessly recurring cycle of birth, nourishment and death.

Salmon carcasses are not the exclusive preserve of the bald eagles. They may be the first and dominant consumer, but they share the bounty in a very specific sequence with gulls and crows. Each of these day-feeders contributes to and benefits from the partnership. Salmon eyes and brains are eaten first, followed by the soft tissue of the entrails. These are drawn out through a hole the size of a cucumber slice. The bald eagle's powerful beak and talons are best suited for ripping apart fish flesh, while the gulls' and crows' beaks are better for probing and picking delectable morsels.

The supply of Squamish salmon is so bountiful that there is also plenty for the night-feeders. Mink, raccoons, coyotes, bobcats, lynx, cougar and black bear — and further upstream, grizzlies — all feast at this age-old restaurant, open 24 hours a day for either eat-in or take-out service. The take-out customers also do their part to enrich the stream. They carry their orders into the woods leaving rotting remains, which fertilize the forest floor — as do eagle leftovers and droppings. The drainage from this enriched soil nourishes the river, which in turn feeds the estuary and eventually the sea.

This complex interplay of eagle and salmon, soil and stream, animal and mineral strengthens the diversity of the valley's environment. Each participant contributes in its kind and benefits as it needs. In this diversity is strength, beauty and even wisdom. When you follow just one thread, the dance of destiny between eagle and salmon, for example, you can see the entire tapestry of life. You can see that the whole is greater than the sum of the parts. To pull out one thread, one part, is to diminish the whole — and to enhance one thread is to strengthen the whole.

For the most part, the natural tapestry of the Squamish Valley is still whole, despite the harvesting

# "My heart soars like an eagle."

CHIEF DAN GEORGE, from the film "Little Big Man"

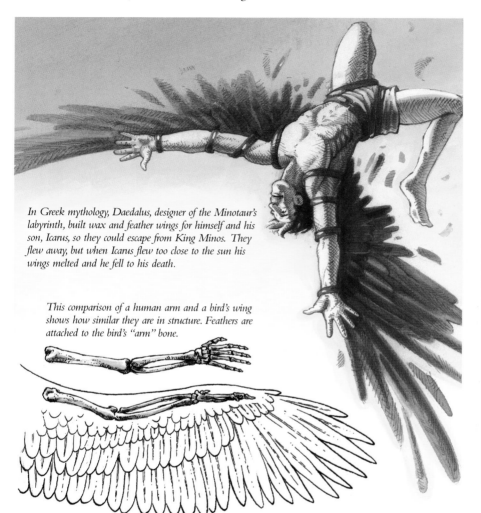

In Greek mythology, Daedalus, designer of the Minotaur's labyrinth, built wax and feather wings for himself and his son, Icarus, so they could escape from King Minos. They flew away, but when Icarus flew too close to the sun his wings melted and he fell to his death.

This comparison of a human arm and a bird's wing shows how similar they are in structure. Feathers are attached to the bird's "arm" bone.

Eagles use their primary feathers at their wing tips to get a steadier ride in strong winds, moving them like we do our fingers. They also use primary feathers when taking off and landing. When diving, bald eagles can reach speeds of 160 kilometres per hour (100 miles per hour). They glide and flap at speeds of 60 - 75 kilometres per hour (35 - 45 miles per hour).

To conserve energy, bald eagles soar on thermals - warm air currents that rise many kilometres from the earth. They use thermals like elevators. If wind pushes a thermal, an eagle will often ride along. When there is no wind, an eagle uses a thermal to circle higher and higher, gliding several kilometres while slowly losing altitude, then rising again on another thermal. Hang-gliders use thermals in exactly the same way.

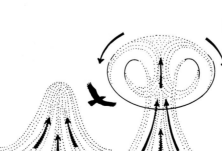

of most of the valley forest, which is now healthy second-growth forest, and the presence of industrial and residential activity for several generations. The eagles came because the habitat was suitable, and that is why they continue to come in ever greater numbers.

The dramatic increase in the number of bald eagles wintering in the valley is directly linked to a significant rise in bald eagle populations in the continental U.S. following the banning of the use of DDT, a pesticide which made their egg shells too thin to protect embryos. The parents often crushed their own offspring. The increase in the number of overwintering bald eagles is also linked to a precipitous decrease in suitable winter habitat in the United States and along the south coast of British Columbia. Large bodies of water are still there, but the tall trees and plentiful supply of fish that bald eagles require have been largely depleted in those regions. There are simply more bald eagles and fewer places for them to survive the winter.

Among the many factors contributing to habitat loss, urban sprawl has been one of the principal culprits. Up to one-third of the salmon spawning populations in southwestern British Columbia have been either lost or severely depleted. But the Squamish system has held its own. So far.

It is no surprise that bald eagles have been coming to the Squamish Valley in ever-increasing numbers. In fact, over the past decade this gathering has become one of the greatest single concentrations of wintering bald eagles in the world. The greatest clusters of bald eagles are closest to heavily wooded Brackendale, where, in 1994, as part of an annual regional survey of eagle populations, more than 150 volunteers counted 3,769 birds — 1,200 more than had ever been counted before. While a scientific survey has yet to be conducted, the count confirmed what appears to be a clear trend toward greater concentrations of overwintering bald eagles in the area.

The numbers in the informal survey put the Squamish River and Brackendale ahead of the world record, also based on an informal count, established at the Chilkat River in Alaska 10 years before. This earned the Canadian community of 3,000 the title of the "world's winter capital for bald eagles." With more bald eagles than people in Brackendale, some volunteers said the skies seemed filled with "clouds of eagles."

The clouds of eagles have set in motion a new cycle, a new dance in which people are starting to learn new steps as partners with salmon and eagle.

FRANK OBERLE

# Paradise

# at Risk

# Paradise at Risk

Like the land and waters, there have been distinct rhythms to the activities of people in the Squamish Valley. But changes now seem to be coming as fast as an eagle flies, threatening the paradise that eagles and others have enjoyed for the past 5,000 years. This sudden shift of tempo is in dramatic counterpoint to the ancient rhythms of the valley.

More than 3,000 years ago the native people, the Sko-Mish, were building their cedar big houses at different sites along the rivers that run through the valley. From Sko-Mish, a name some say means "birthplace of the winds," came Squamish. From the Sko-Mish people also comes a way of understanding the valley based on intimate knowledge of the ways of all creatures which share the land and water.

For thousands of years the Sko-Mish fished streams rich with salmon and oolichan, hunted in forests plentiful with deer, moose and elk and collected plants, roots, berries and seeds from the forest and rich delta soils. They travelled and traded widely in the interior and on the coast, all the while staying true to traditions passed from generation to generation.

It was a way of life that had already undergone wrenching change when Squamish hereditary chief Alvie Andrew was a boy at the turn of the century.

Yet he still hunted birds with bows and arrows and fished rivers so thick with salmon he could easily spear them and flip the silver-scaled fish to land. As this century closes, he sees that while much has changed around him, some things will never change.

"The salmon and the eagle and us people are all the same," says Andrew. "We all need places where we can live, where there is food, where we can raise our children. So much is so different from when I was young. The dirt track is now a highway. Where this house stands was once a swamp. But long after you and I are gone, the eagle, the salmon and people will still need the same things."

The arrival of European settlers late in the 19th-century brought new needs, and new ways of meeting them. Over a century of booms and busts the settlers built farms, logged the forests, built cattle trails and commercial fisheries. They built mines, sawmills, pulp mills and ports, and established villages and towns that eventually became the District Municipality of Squamish. The railroads and highways that finally linked the valley to Vancouver in the 1950s made it much easier for people from afar to discover the valley as a place of stunning natural beauty — and a versatile playground.

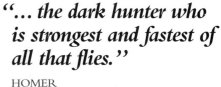

## "... the dark hunter who is strongest and fastest of all that flies."

HOMER

*The famous painter and illustrator John James Audubon both painted the bald eagle and described its opportunistic ways: "Many vultures were feeding on the carcass of a dead horse when the sudden appearance of an eagle put them all to flight, one amongst the rest with a portion of the entrails partly swallowed, and the remaining part, about a yard in length, dangling in the air. The eagle instantly marked him and gave chase. The poor vulture tried in vain to disgorge, when the eagle, coming up, seized the loose end of the gut and dragged the bird along for 20 or 30 yards, much against its will, until both fell to the ground when the eagle struck the vulture and in a few moments killed it, after which he swallowed his delicious morsel."*

*Bald eagles are superb hunters - when they have to be. A meat eater, the bald eagle must catch and kill all it eats, or find flesh that has already been killed. Scavenging is the bald eagle's preferred method of finding food. They are masters at pirating - stealing from other eagles, and kleptoparasitism - stealing from other species, especially osprey.*

*A Plains warrior's shield, made of buffalo hide hardened by steam and smoke, was tough enough to stop an arrow or deflect a lance. Just as warriors invoked supernatural powers through prayers and songs while making shields, so too did hunters call upon animal spirits before setting out on the hunt.*

Today the Squamish Valley is experiencing another stage in its evolution, as the forest industry that anchors the local economy undergoes profound change. People fear government reductions in the amount of timber made available for logging will mean fewer jobs, diminished prosperity and a very different flavour to the life of the community; yet people hope this challenge also represents an opportunity to further diversify an economy already in transformation.

Over the past two decades the pace of development in the valley has quickened in sync with the spectacular growth of metropolitan Vancouver to the south and Whistler to the north. Families seeking breathing space have started to inflate the population and make Squamish another bedroom community for Vancouver. At the same time, the swift rise of Whistler as an international resort is bringing more visitors to and through the Squamish Valley. The highway linking Vancouver and Whistler passes through the valley, and there are now proposals to boost tourism by expanding both the highway and service to the airport, which is located at the edge of Brackendale.

Visitors come to the valley to camp, to ride the rapids on the mountain rivers, or the antique steam train, to fish and to climb the bare rock faces of the valley walls. They are also coming, in the thousands, to see the "clouds of eagles."

Many who live and work in the Squamish Valley have been involved in the annual gathering of bald eagles. For more than 20 years, Brackendale Art Gallery founder and proprietor Thor Froslev has watched the number of wintering eagles, and eagle watchers, grow steadily. He has been a driving force in making people more aware of the bird's presence, promoting the annual bald eagle count and Brackendale Eagle Festival and attempting to establish a reserve to protect their habitat. Now urban sprawl, industrial activity and the growing numbers of eagle watchers must be better integrated and managed so they won't become threats to bald eagle habitat.

"People are coming here from across the continent because they want to experience the wonder of these creatures," says Froslev. "I saw a man from Boston stand weeping as he gazed on a tree full of bald eagles. This is a precious part of life. If we don't act now to protect habitat, we risk losing the bald eagles forever. There are fewer and fewer places left for them to go in winter in southern British Columbia."

Froslev's work is closely allied to that of the Squamish Estuary Conservation Society, which has applied to the provincial government to establish a 1,500-hectare bald eagle reserve along the river. The group's treasurer, Len "Lefty" Goldsmith, is a lifelong area resident, a retired machinist and an avid outdoors-

CAROL FUEGI

*"The clinching interlocking claws,*
*a living fierce gyrating wheel,*
*Four beating wings, two beaks,*
*a swirling mass tight grappling,*
*In tumbling turning clustering loops,*
*straight downward falling,*
*Till o'er the river pois'd,*
*the twain yet one,*
*a moment's lull*
*a motionless still balance in the air,*
*then parting, talons loosing,*
*Upward again*
*on slow-firm pinions slanting,*
*their separate diverse flight,*
*She hers, he his, pursuing."*

from "The Dalliance of Eagles"
by WALT WHITMAN

FRANK OBERLE

To Walt Whitman, the sky dancing of eagles was poetry in air; to scientists, it is a talon grapple. But no one is certain why eagles engage in this double cartwheeling that dazzles those lucky enough to witness it. Most believe the movements are a courtship display, one of the most elaborate of any raptor. It may well be, for the airborne intertwining seems a prelude of togetherness to come. Most scientists also believe that eagles pair for life. Usually eagles find mates at about age five, but only one in 10 survives to that age.

**Approach**          **The Dance**          **Release**

man who knows these woods and waters as well as anyone in the valley.

To him, protecting the kinds of trees the eagles need is as critical as protecting the rivers. Goldsmith says a protected area would benefit not only eagles, but also trumpeter swans, great blue herons, hummingbirds, kingfishers, ducks and other wildlife.

Another local institution, the North Vancouver Outdoor School, a part of the public school system, is also keenly attuned to the web of life that supports salmon, eagle and people. Since its inception in 1969, the school has worked to enhance salmon and eagle habitat with strong support from the Department of Fisheries and Oceans and other groups. The school's prime function is hands-on environmental education that enhances people's understanding of how they can become better integrated into life's tapestry.

"We have a living library here," says the school's principal, Victor Elderton. "The land, water and wildlife form a complex, fragile and wondrous web that changes every day. When we follow the changes of plant and animal life, we learn to change how we understand the world and our place in it."

Like Froslev, Goldsmith and many others in the valley, Elderton knows that time is becoming a critical factor. The rising popularity of the eagles — and the consequent disturbance that the viewing public repre-

sents — is a potential threat to the overwintering eagle population. Unrestricted public access to the bald eagles wintering areas is already having an effect. Observers have noted that when eagle watchers are out in force, eagles vacate the area — and return when people leave. Most visitors come on weekends, so the disturbance is greatest then. There is concern that people will start coming during the week to avoid the crowds, and so extend the time eagles are subjected to human intrusion. And there are further concerns about the potential effects of increased air traffic, housing development, the expansion of Squamish port facilities and the logging of private timberlands on prime eagle habitat.

The Outdoor School had a further concern about its own future in connection with continued funding at a time when school boards across the region were looking for ways to cut costs. Its own habitat, in the form of a lease-to-own agreement on the school's 165 hectare (420 acre) site near Brackendale, was facing a potential challenge. By chance Elderton saw an ad by The Nature Conservancy of Canada. The ad invited concerned Canadians to call a toll-free number if they wanted to help preserve Canada's wild places.

Elderton called. The Nature Conservancy entered the picture, inaugurating another cycle of change in the valley — and bringing new hope to the eagles of Brackendale.

Protection in

# Perpetuity

# Protection in Perpetuity

Victor Elderton's call to the Nature Conservancy has opened a window of opportunity for not only the eagles of Brackendale, but also for individuals and groups in the Squamish Valley, across British Columbia and Canada, and indeed, around the world.

In many ways, the Nature Conservancy's involvement marks a watershed in the way this national charity is helping save Canada's wild places while there's still time.

After the phone call and subsequent contacts and visits to the Squamish Valley, The Conservancy conducted a thorough evaluation, as it has done for each of the 600 preserves it has already helped establish across the country. Establishing these preserves generally involved focusing protection on a single species, purchasing either a single or a few pieces of readily identified property, securing financial support from a number of private sources and involving a local group or government ministry in long-term stewardship that would maintain natural values. As a rule, it has all been done quietly, behind the scenes.

In the Squamish Valley, the challenge and the response are different, says Kirk Davis, Director of the Nature Conservancy in British Columbia.

"We're looking at multiple species, including salmon, eagles and various trees; and there is no single property, but a patchwork throughout the valley — many of them in the midst of homes, businesses and industrial sites," Davis explains. "We also have a multitude of interests to consider, including biodiversity, First Nations, urban development, and the forest industry, tourism and transportation."

For many, this apparent conflict among interests is a tremendous opportunity to guide the evolution of the valley in ways that enhance both the environment and the economy. At least that's the way Meg Fellowes, Squamish District Municipality councillor, sees the situation.

"On the estuary we still have overwintering waterfowl right next to log-booming grounds, a yacht club and major trucking activity; it's a unique juxtaposition, and we know it's possible," Fellowes says. "Whether we want it or not, people will be coming from all over to see the eagles here, probably in overwhelming numbers. We have to plan very carefully how to protect and enhance this ancient part of our ecology while it becomes a new part of our economy."

CAMERON HERYET/IMAGE NETWORK

## "And we (being in love) in us find the eagle and the dove."

JOHN DUNNE

*A bald eagle pair make an eyrie, or eagle nest, of sticks, branches, bark, and weeds, with the female doing most of the building. The couple use the nest year after year, and often build back-up nests as well. Bald eagle nests are the largest bird nests in North America, often found in old-growth trees. One nest in northern California measured six metres (20 ft) deep and three metres (10 ft) across the top. It weighed 2,700 kg (6,000 lbs).*

*Bald eagle couples line the nest with feathers, soft greenery and needles from evergreens, forming a slight hollow in the centre for eggs. They also decorate the top edge with greenery, perhaps to signal to other eagles that the nest is occupied.*

WAYNE LYNCH

*In the Roman army, each unit had a standard; the standard of a legion was the aquila, or eagle. The legions believed a site was suitable for winter quarters if an eagle's eyrie was nearby.*

### Four Shapes of the Eagle's Nest

**Cylindrical**

**Bowl**

**Inverted Cone**

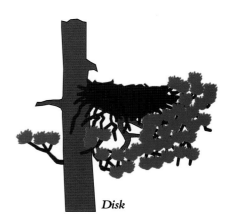

**Disk**

Fortunately the Nature Conservancy has some new tools, as well as strong financial commitments that will help make the most of this opportunity. In 1994, a new provincial law enabled third parties such as The Conservancy to hold and enforce conservation covenants registered on land titles. This was previously the exclusive province of government. These conservation covenants may prove an invaluable addition to outright land acquisition in protecting salmon and eagle habitat on the patchwork of properties in the valley.

To date, the funding the Nature Conservancy has secured for the eagles of Brackendale marks a departure from its traditional practice of cultivating support from a number of organizations. Early on, it became clear that substantial resources would be needed for so ambitious a project. It also became clear that there was very strong interest in providing initial financial support for the project from a single source — the Forest Alliance of British Columbia.

The Forest Alliance is a coalition of British Columbians from all areas of the province and all walks of life whose common concern is to protect B.C.'s forest environment and forest-based economy. The Alliance's mission is to find ways to achieve both environmental protection and economic stability in the use of the province's forest resources. Getting involved in the eagles of Brackendale project also marks the start of moving in a new direction for the Alliance, says Chairman Jack Munro.

"It is part of moving away from confrontation and reaction toward proactive cooperation," Munro says. "The forest industry is changing and it affects all of us. We're turning to multiple use, learning to balance environmental and economic realities. The Nature Conservancy has a great track record of being able to deal with complex issues and work with all parties. We feel working together with them is a perfect fit for the Forest Alliance's new direction."

For Munro, the support will be more than just financial.

"There is a lot of know-how in the Alliance. There is also a lot we can contribute as a hands-on partner."

While the extent, type and administration of the preserve have yet to be identified, a few essentials are clear, says the Nature Conservancy's Davis. The financial support of the Forest Alliance is crucial to secure and protect land and critical salmon spawning areas on which eagles depend. The acquisition and protection of land has proven itself time and again, perhaps most notably along the Chilkat River near Haines, Alaska. The first significant parcel of land that will become part of a nature preserve has already been identified: the 165 hectare (420 acre) North Vancouver Outdoor School site.

Wildlife biologists Barry Booth and Markus Merkens have conducted research on bald eagles in the Squamish watershed for the Nature Conservancy. They believe that maintaining bald eagles in the Brackendale area will require integrating bald eagle biology with forest management and urban development outside an eagle reserve, as well as controlling access to the wintering areas. This kind of approach would allow the public to experience these regal raptors in a setting that simultaneously promotes understanding, protects their winter habitat and contributes to their health and survival.

# *"Like an eagle that stirs up its nest, that flutters over its young, spreading out its wings, catching them, bearing them in its pinions..."*

DEUTERONOMY 32: 11

TOM & PAT LEESON/DRK PHOTO

The first eaglet to hatch is fed first. Fighting often erupts, and can be lethal to younger eaglets. There are two to three feedings a day and eaglets can get more than 50 bits of food in a single 10-minute feeding. The bald eagle is one of the fastest growing birds in North America. In six weeks, eaglets are 40 times their birth weight. If a human baby grew as fast, in six weeks, he or she would weigh more than 136 kg (300 lbs).

Clutch: One to three eggs, usually two
Incubation: 31-46 days
Eggs turned every hour

At six to seven weeks, eaglets start eating on their own; at 10 to 12 weeks, they have all their feathers and can leave the nest. Usually young eagles just start flapping their wings and fly. After a few months they become adept hunters. Then they are ready to leave the nesting area and migrate to winter habitat. Head and tail feathers start turning white when the birds are three years old; by age seven, they're fully mature, and head and tail feathers are completely white.

Bald eagles are attentive parents. During incubation, both male and female lose the feathers on a small patch on the lower breast. This area has a rich supply of blood vessels that transfer heat to the eggs. The female does most of the incubating, and eggs are rarely left alone.

FRANK OBERLE

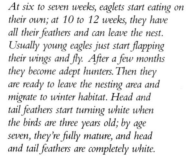

Bald eagle eggs are small in comparison to the size of the bird.

**3 days**

FRANK OBERLE

**8 weeks**

FRANK OBERLE

**1–2 years**

S. NEILSEN/DRK PHOTO

**Fully Mature**

FRANK OBERLE

CAMERON HERVET/IMAGE NETWORK

"Being involved in this sort of management will be new territory for us," adds Davis. "But there is an enormous amount of knowledge, concern and willingness among so many different groups to work together for change. The Conservancy is really more of a catalyst in a process that is attempting to provide protection in perpetuity."

The final way the eagles of Brackendale project breaks new ground for the Nature Conservancy is that it will become a very public affair. This book is the first step in informing people of what has been done to date and of the hurdles to come. From this point forward, people's interest and energy for the eagles could swell into a river of support. And this river, enriched by understanding, could become as important to the survival of these eagles as the annual return of salmon.

The intimate connection between eagle and human is something the people of the Squamish Nation have always known. To them, the salmon and eagle are people, just as you and I are people, according to Aaron Nelson-Moody, who helps develop native curriculum for the Squamish Nation.

"We treat them with respect, as we would another human being," says Nelson-Moody, whose native name is Tawk-sin Yeqwulla, or Splashing Young Eagle. "This is a shared space. When we enter their part of the space, we do so with the eagles' leave and on their terms."

People are becoming aware of the rhythms of the land beneath them. They feel more deeply the connection between themselves, the salmon in the river and the eagles in the sky. And they are seeing that the window of opportunity is open.

The time to act is now. The place to act is here. The eagles of Brackendale are coming. May they always return. And may they always find people who treat them with respect.

RUSS HEINL/IMAGE NETWORK

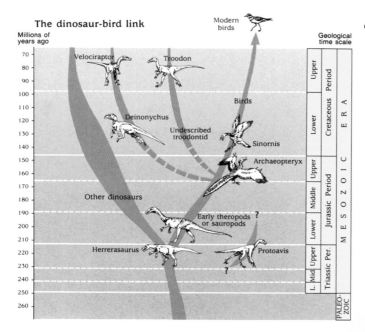

The dinosaur-bird link

Millions of years ago

| | Geological time scale |
|---|---|

# "Take a bird and pluck the feathers off and you have a dinosaur"

PHILIP CURRIE, Paleontologist

*Most dinosaurs disappeared 65 million years ago, but some of the smaller ones winged their way into the future, according to Philip Currie, author of The Flying Dinosaurs and director of the dinosaur research program at the Royal Tyrell Museum of Paleontology in Drumheller, Alberta. It's a theory he shares with Robert Bakker, a U.S. paleontologist and author of The Dinosaur Heresies. They challenge a long-held view that dinosaurs and birds shared the same ancestors. Instead, they suggest, birds actually descended from dinosaurs.*

Archaeopteryx-
the earliest bird

*Currie and Bakker cite more than 100 similarities between dinosaurs and birds, including: warm bloodedness, brain capability, foot structure, social group function, annual migrations and rearing of their young.*

*A sketch of the hypothetical "Proavis," proposed by some scientists as a tree-dwelling ancestor to Archaeopteryx and modern birds. Proavis was thought to have glided rather than flown, with scales eventually evolving into feathers.*

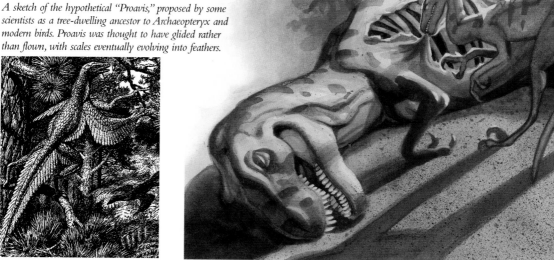

# The Nature Conservancy of Canada

The Nature Conservancy of Canada is the only national charity dedicated to purchasing areas of ecological significance, outstanding beauty and educational interest in order to protect biodiversity.

The Nature Conservancy focuses on the most threatened ecosystems in Canada, those in which only a fraction of the original habitat remains. The beaches, woodlands, wetlands, and prairies The Conservancy acquires include important wildlife sanctuaries, environmental education areas, the last traces of wilderness near urban centres or lands that are symbols of our country's natural splendour. These lands have been identified as high priorities for preservation by a national network of scientific advisors.

The properties the Nature Conservancy purchases are permanently protected as nature preserves, parks, public recreation areas, wildlife and forest management areas, ranches and historic or archaeological sites.

The Conservancy brings about the conservation of natural land on a meaningful scale by combining three critical components: science, real estate skills and financial resources. The Nature Conservancy's acquisitions are based on building partnerships, applying real estate expertise and developing creative stewardship strategies. The Conservancy works with a variety of sources — individuals, corporations, communities and governments — to assemble capital to secure privately owned natural lands. Taking a cue from the infinite variety of nature, The Conservancy takes a flexible approach to structuring acquisitions that conserve these natural, national treasures. The Nature Conservancy takes pride in working with business and thanking their partners publicly.

The results of this approach speak for themselves. Since its founding in 1962, the Nature Conservancy has established some 600 nature preserves, helping to protect more than 494,543 hectares (1,222,000 acres) within Canada. The contributions of some 20,000 donors nationwide have now made it possible to accelerate the pace of protection. Since 1990, The Conservancy has raised more than $37 million for conservation. Today, The Conservancy establishes a new nature preserve every two weeks.

IMAGES B.C./IMAGE NETWORK

FRANK OBERLE

# "They that wait upon the lord shall renew their strength; they shall be mount up with wings as eagles"

ISAIAH, 40:31

*"I wish the bald eagle had not been chosen as the representative of our country. He is a bird of bad moral character, like those among men who live by sharping and robbing, he is very often poor and very often lousy."*

*Benjamin Franklin, founding father of the United States of America*

Early settlers regarded bald eagles as pests; they shot and poisoned them, and ruined their habitat by clearing the land, building dams and polluting waterways. By the early 20th-century the bald eagle began to disappear from much of its range in the U.S. In the late 1940s and 1950s, water pollution was becoming a serious problem. In particular, the pesticide DDT began working its way through the food chain and into the fish that bald eagles ate. By the 1960s, it had caused such a dramatic decline in bald eagle reproduction that they were believed to be on the brink of extinction in the continental United States. DDT was eventually banned and bald eagle populations recovered so strongly that their status was upgraded from endangered to threatened. Pollution and development, however, still remain significant threats to bald eagles.

*"A bird neither beautiful nor musical nor good for food, but murderous, greedy, hateful to all, the curse of all and with its great power of doing harm only surpassed by its desire to do it."*

*Erasmus, Dutch Renaissance scholar referring to the eagle*

The deadly link between DDT and bald eagle reproduction was first identified by a retired Canadian bank manager and amateur ornithologist, Charles Broley.

Estimated★ North American bald eagle population, 1600 A.D. to 2000 A.D.

500,000

400,000

300,000

200,000

100,000

1600 A.D.    1700 A.D.    1800 A.D.    1900 A.D.

CAMERON HERYET/IMAGE NETWORK

★ based on compilation from various sources.

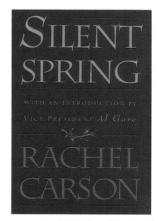

In 1962, the publication of Rachel Carson's Silent Spring alerted the world to the extent and dangers of pollution to both wildlife and people.

# The Nature Conservancy of Canada in British Columbia

The Nature Conservancy launched its efforts in B.C. in 1972. Over the past 23 years, The Conservancy has helped establish 31 nature preserves comprising some 12,249 hectares (30,068 acres) throughout British Columbia. These preserves protect some of B.C.'s most threatened natural areas: wetlands, old-growth forests, grasslands and coastal habitats such as the Gulf Islands.

The first project involved working with other interests to secure 59 hectares (145 acres) of wetland habitat at Mud Bay/Boundary Bay. Located in the Fraser River Estuary just south of Vancouver, Boundary Bay has both national and ecological significance as an area for migratory birds and many other species of wildlife.

A variety of conservation projects soon followed, many of them cooperative efforts with communities in the Gulf Islands. Whole islands, and parts of islands, have been purchased and are now protected for scientific research, educational use and the preservation of natural biological diversity.
- Cabbage Island (4 hectares/11 acres) in 1978.
- Sidney Island (42 hectares/105 acres) in 1979.
- Brackman Island (5 hectares/12 acres) in 1988.

- Galiano Island (17 hectares/42 acres) in 1990; very rare B.C. habitat of dry coastal Douglas fir forest and the south-facing cliffs of Mt. Sutil.
- Read Island (9 hectares/22 acres); forest habitat preserving a pocket of old-growth fir and cedar.
- Quadra Island (23 hectares/57 acres) at Morte Lake. Four different ecological communities, including endangered coastal Douglas fir, are represented.

Partnership has been critical to The Conservancy's success in securing natural habitats throughout the province. The most recent example is the Commonwealth Nature Legacy Park, a 1,057 hectare (2,612 acre) dry coastal Douglas fir forest bordered by eight kilometres of pristine ocean shoreline. The Mount Broadwood Heritage Conservation Area in southeastern British Columbia represented Canada's largest private conservation project in 1992. The 8,944 hectares (22,100 acres) in the Conservation Area has the greatest abundance and diversity of large mammals on private land in North America — including grizzly bear, elk, bighorn sheep, wolves and cougars.

CAMERON HERYET/IMAGE NETWORK

> *"Screaming the night away with his great wing feathers,*
> *Swooping the darkness up, I hear the eagle bird*
> *Pulling the blanket back off from the eastern sky."*
>
> IROQUOIS INVITATION SONG

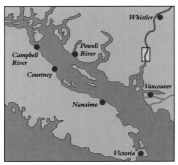

*To get to Squamish and Brackendale from Vancouver, drive north on Hwy. 99, the Sea-to Sky Highway, a spectacular 75-kilometre drive along Howe Sound. Brackendale is 8 kilometres north of Squamish. From Whistler, follow Hwy. 99 south.*

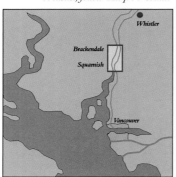

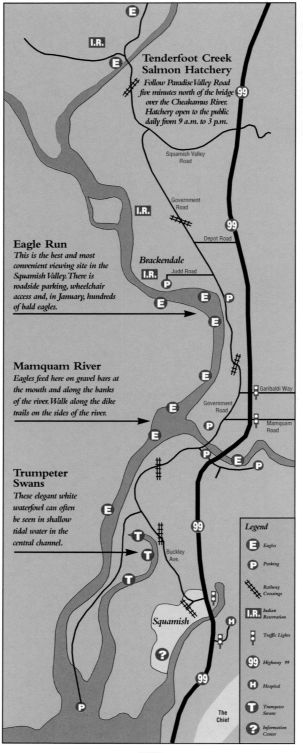

**Tenderfoot Creek Salmon Hatchery**
*Follow Paradise Valley Road five minutes north of the bridge over the Cheakamus River. Hatchery open to the public daily from 9 a.m. to 3 p.m.*

**Eagle Run**
*This is the best and most convenient viewing site in the Squamish Valley. There is roadside parking, wheelchair access and, in January, hundreds of bald eagles.*

**Mamquam River**
*Eagles feed here on gravel bars at the mouth and along the banks of the river. Walk along the dike trails on the sides of the river.*

**Trumpeter Swans**
*These elegant white waterfowl can often be seen in shallow tidal water in the central channel.*

**Legend**

| | |
|---|---|
| **E** | *Eagles* |
| **P** | *Parking* |
| ## | *Railway Crossings* |
| **I.R.** | *Indian Reservation* |
| | *Traffic Lights* |
| **99** | *Highway 99* |
| **H** | *Hospital* |
| **T** | *Trumpeter Swans* |
| **?** | *Information Center* |

**Please Do Not Disturb**

*Wintering eagles need to feed often and conserve energy to survive the cold and wet. Winter is especially hard on younger eagles who are still growing. People making noise and tramping through their feeding and resting areas, and the sound of motorboats upset the eagles and make them burn up precious energy. Please keep your distance. Respect the eagles' need for peace and quiet. And please respect private property.*

**Choosing a Visiting Site**

*There are several good sites for viewing eagles. Eagle Run is the most convenient and one of the most popular. The Mamquam River is another favourite spot. You can walk on trails on the dike on both sides of Highway 99 and see eagles on the gravel bars and perched in the trees. If you follow Paradise Valley Road about five minutes north of the bridge over the Cheakamus River at Cheekeye, you will come to Tenderfoot Creek Hatchery, a great spot for seeing eagles, salmon, heron and ducks.*

# The Forest Alliance of British Columbia

The Forest Alliance of B.C. is a coalition of British Columbians from all areas of the province and all walks of life whose common concern is to protect B.C.'s forest environment and forest-based economy. The mission of the Alliance is to find ways to achieve both environmental protection and economic stability in the use of British Columbia's forest resources.

The purpose of the Forest Alliance is to provide a mechanism through which the interests of British Columbians, concerned with maintaining a healthy forest environment and forest-based economy, can be coordinated and be represented to government, industry and the public.

The Alliance provides British Columbians with information on the current state of B.C.'s forest practices and forest environment, and indicates where improvement is needed to ensure the long-term health and productivity of both the forest industry and the forest environment.

## Goals
- to create a broad-based membership of people who support protecting the forest environment and maintaining the forest industry as a means of ensuring a diverse and stable economy for British Columbia.
- to provide educational programs, seminars and special projects to improve British Columbians awareness of what is taking place in their forests.
- to identify issues in the use of B.C.'s forest land and forest resources that members of the Alliance feel require attention and to communicate the facts and various perspectives on these issues to British Columbians.

- to make recommendations to industry, government and other forest-sector groups on issues pertaining to B.C.'s forest resources, their planning, management and use.
- to provide a vehicle and forum for dialogue among the various stakeholders in British Columbia's forest lands.

## Structure

Directed by a Citizens Board of approximately 30 British Columbians representing various communities and different points of view, the Alliance provides a broad perspective on forestry issues.

Through a variety of activities, including commissioned studies, and fact-finding missions, the Alliance investigates and communicates facts surrounding forest issues. Through seminars, community forums and publications, the Alliance supports dialogue on land use.

KHAREN HILL/IMAGE NETWORK

# A Gallery of Eagles

*Bald Eagle With Salmon,* Robert Bateman

Wherever the eagle ranges — and that is the whole world except Antarctica — it has become a symbol on which the imagination soars. The art and artifacts on these pages are meant to be a mere sampling of the ways the eagle has opened eyes, and minds, over millennia. People naturally develop an affinity for the types of eagle with whom they share the land, sea and sky. In the Pacific Northwest, it is the bald eagle that gives wing to the imagination of native and newcomer alike.

# A Gallery of Eagles

*The Bald Eagle,* John James Audubon
Collection of the New–York Historical Society

# A Gallery of Eagles

*Eagle Bulging Bent Bowl,* Larry Rosso,
Gallery of Tribal Art

*Eagle Grease Bowl,* Wilfred Sampson (Gitksan),
Douglas Reynolds Gallery

*Eagles Pole,* Richard Hunt,
Gallery of Tribal Art

*Nisroch was an eagle-headed god of
ancient Assyria. Eagle gods were common in ancient Mesopotamia. The
Babylonian god of fertility, storm and
war was another eagle god, Ningursu.*

# A Gallery of Eagles

*A representation of Garuda from Thailand. Garuda is a bird-king from ancient Indian scriptures. This implacable enemy of serpents carried Vishnu, a member of the Hindu trinity who often took on human form, most notably as Krishna. The Garuda is a familiar image across southeast Asia.*

*Eagle Belt Buckle,* Henry Green, Gallery of Tribal Art

*Split Eagle Design Ring,* Norman Bentley, Gallery of Tribal Art

*Eagle Bracelet,* Henry Green, Gallery of Tribal Art

*Eagle,* Silkscreen Print, Larry Rosso
Douglas Reynolds Gallery

# A Gallery of Eagles

*Eagle Transforming into Itself,* Robert Davidson

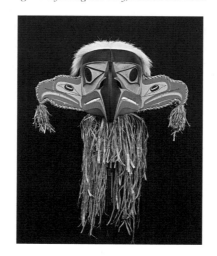

# A Gallery of Eagles

*Eagle About to Take Flight,* artist unknown, Meiji Period, Japan, 1868 – 1912

# A Gallery of Eagles

*This artwork is the creation of well-known Coast Salish artist Richard Krentz, one of the Shi'sha'lh (Sechelt) nation. The artist's style reflects a strong faith in his creator. Whether his images are carved in cedar or painted on wood or paper, they portray qualities of hope, joy, peace and love.*

*The Eagle watches over all creation. The Eagle is the protector of the home and is the symbol of wisdom and vision.*

*The Nature Conservancy of Canada is grateful for Richard's generous gift of this original art to our Eagles of Brackendale conservation effort.*

*The Squamish people tell this story to celebrate the rhythm of life that brings the salmon to their waters. Without the return of the salmon, there would be no return of the eagles to the valley.*

## Why the Salmon Came to the Squamish Waters

Long ago when animals and human beings were the same, there were four brothers who went about doing good. They usually travelled on the water, in a canoe. This was not an ordinary canoe; it was really the youngest of the four brothers transformed into that shape.

Coming to the Squamish one time, they were persuaded by the chief to stay a while in his village. Knowing the wonder-working powers of the brothers, the chief said to them, "Won't you bring the salmon people to our shores? We are often short of food. We know that salmon is good, but they never come to our waters."

"We will persuade the salmon people," replied the oldest brother, "if we can find out where they live. We shall have to ask Snookum, the sun."

But it was difficult to get near enough to the sun to ask him anything. He was a wily creature and seldom left the sky. The brothers knew that they would have to use craft to bring him down After much pondering and discussion, they transformed the youngest brother into a salmon and tied him to the shore with a fishing line. By sporting about in the water, the salmon attracted the attention of Snookum. But before doing anything, the sun also used craft; he caused the three brothers to go into a deep trance. Then in the form of an eagle, Snookum descended from the sky, pounced upon the salmon and flew away with it, breaking the line as he flew.

When the three brothers awakened from their trance, they used their wonder-working powers again. They transformed their third brother into a whale and tied him to the shore. This time they used a rope, which was stouter than the line they had used for the salmon. Again the sun cast the brothers into a trance and descended from the sky in the form of an eagle. He fixed his claws firmly into the flesh of the floating whale and started aloft with it. This time the rope did not break. Again and again the eagle tried to break it, but he could not. Neither could he free his claws from the whale's flesh.

While he was still struggling, the two brothers awoke from their trance. They pulled the whale

*The Salmon Chief*

to shore, dragging the sun with it. They said to Snookum, "Don't struggle, my friend. You cannot get away without our help, and we will not give it to you unless you do what we ask you to do."

Knowing that they had outwitted him, Sun-Eagle struggled no more with the whale. "What do you want me to do," he asked?

"Tell us where the salmon people live," said the oldest brother. "You can see all over the world when you are up in the sky."

"The home of the salmon is a long way off in that direction," replied the Sun, pointing toward the west. "If you want to visit them, you must first prepare much medicine and take it with you. Then all will be well."

The brother released Sun-Eagle, and he flew off into the clouds. After gathering many herbs and making much medicine, they said to the Squamish people, "Get out your canoes and make ready for a long journey. At sunrise tomorrow we will set out for a visit with the salmon people."

Next morning they all started westward. For many days they paddled, and finally they came near an island. But they could not get close to its shore because of a large amount of floating charcoal. One of the Squamish youth tried to walk on it, but it gave way beneath his feet and he drowned. Paddling around the charcoal, they went to the other side of the island. There they saw what seemed to be a village. Smoke of all colours rose into the clouds.

"This seems to be the country we are looking for," said the brothers. "Sun told us that this is the home of the salmon people."

So the paddlers took the canoes to the beach, which was very broad and smooth. All the Squamish people went toward the village, the four brothers carrying the medicine with them. They gave some of the medicine to the Spring Salmon, the chief of the village. As a result, he was friendly toward the whole party.

In the stream behind the village, Spring Salmon kept a fish trap. Shortly before the visitors had landed, the chief had directed four of his young people, two boys and two girls, to go into the water and swim up the creek into the salmon trap. Obeying his orders, they had drawn their blankets up over their heads and walked into the sea. As soon as the water reached their faces, they became salmon. They leaped and played together, just as the salmon do in the running season, and frolicked their way toward the trap in the creek.

So when the time came to welcome the strangers with a feast, Chief Spring Salmon ordered others of his people to go to the salmon trap, bring back the four fish they would find there, and clean and roast them for the guests. The visitors watched the villagers clean the four salmon, cut them open, and spread them above the flames on a kind of wooden gridiron. When the salmon were cooked, the chief invited his guests to eat.

"Eat all you wish," he said, "but do not throw away any of the bones. Be sure to lay them aside carefully. Do not destroy even a small bone."

The Squamish and the brothers gladly accepted the invitation, partook freely of the roasted salmon, but wondered why they were asked to save the bones.

When all had finished eating, some of the young men of the salmon village carefully picked up the little pile of bones the guests had made, took them to the beach, and threw them into the sea. A few minutes later the four young people who had earlier gone into the water reappeared and joined the others. For four days the Chief thus entertained his guests with salmon feasts.

The care taken with the bones at each meal excited the curiosity of one of the visitors. On the fourth day, he secretly kept back some of the bones and hid them. At the close of the meal, the rest of the salmon bones were collected in the usual manner and cast into the sea. Immediately afterwards, four young people came out of the water. But one of them, the visitors noticed, was covering his face with his hands.

Approaching Kos, the salmon chief, the youth said, "Not all of the bones were collected. I do not have any for my cheeks and nose."

Turning to his guests, Kos asked, "Did any of you mislay any of your salmon bones? Some are missing." And he pointed to the face of the young man.

Alarmed by the result of his act, the Squamish youth who had hidden the bones brought them out, pretending that he had just found them on the ground. Now all the visitors were certain that their hosts were the salmon people.

Some time later a large number of seagulls were seen gathering about an object that floated on the water a little distance from the shore.

"Go out and see what is attracting the gulls," Chief Kos directed one of his young men.

Soon the man returned and reported that it was the body of the Squamish youth who, the visitors said, had sunk beneath the floating charcoal on the other side of the island. When the body was brought ashore, it was discovered that the eyes were missing.

The four brothers had the power to restore a body to life, but they could not restore lost eyes.

"Can you supply a new pair of eyes?" they asked the salmon chief. Kos replied that he could and offered a pair of eyes from a Sockeye salmon. They were too small. Then he offered a pair of Coho eyes. They also were too small. Then he selected a pair of Dog-salmon eyes. They were exactly the right size. The oldest of the four brothers sprinkled the body with some of the medicine they had brought, and the youth came to life again. All was well.

"We have come to visit you, Chief Kos, for a special purpose," explained the oldest brother. "We came to ask you to let some of your salmon people visit Squamish waters and come up the streams of the Squamish people. My friends are poor, and they often go hungry. We shall be very grateful if your people will sometimes visit them."

"I will do as you request," replied the salmon chief, "on one condition: they must throw all the salmon bones back into the water as you have seen us do. If they will be careful with the bones, my people can return to us again after they visit you."

"We promise," said the four brothers.

"We promise" said all the Squamish people.

Then they made preparations to return to their home across the water, toward the rising sun.

As they were leaving, the salmon chief said, "I will send Spring salmon to you first in the season. After them I will send Sockeye, then the Coho, then the Dog-salmon and last of all the Humpback."

Ever since that time, long ago, different kinds of salmon, in that order, have come to the Squamish waters — to the sea, into the straits, and into the streams. And in the days of old, before the coming of white people, the Squamish were always very careful to throw the bones of the salmon back into the water.

The efforts and generous contributions of the following have helped make this project possible for The Nature Conservancy of Canada.

Forest Alliance of British Columbia
P.O. Box 49312 - 1055 Dunsmuir Street
Vancouver, British Columbia, Canada   V7X 1L3
Tel: (604) 685-7507    Toll-free: 1-800-567-TREE    Fax: (604) 685-5373
WWW address:  http://www.forest.org

Concept and Creative Direction: Gary McCartie

Text: Patrick Cotter

Coordination and Photo Editing: Trudy Woodcock

Art Direction: Jim Donoahue

Design and Production: Creative Spirit Communications - Dean Landstad and Melissa Moskal

Illustrations: James Bowes and Michael McCartie

Photography:

| | | |
|---|---|---|
| Owen Broad | Al Harvey | Thomas Kitchen |
| Jamie Drouin | Russ Heinl | Tom & Pat Leeson |
| DRK Photo | Bob Herger | Wayne Lynch |
| Gary Fiegehen | Cameron Heryet | S. Nielson |
| First Light | Kharen Hill | Frank Oberle |
| Carol Fuegi | Images B.C. | Graham Osborne |
| | Image Network | |

Printing: Quebecor Printing Vancouver

Paper and Cover Stock: Island Paper Mills

Colour Separations and Film: WYSIWYG Prepress Inc., Vancouver

Binding: Coast Trade Bindery

Acknowledgements:

Page 52    *Bald Eagle With Salmon,* Robert Bateman, ©1972 Boshkung, Inc.
reproduction rights courtesy of Boshkung, Inc.

Page 57    *Eagle About to Take Flight,* courtesy Uno Langmann Ltd., photo by Jamie Drouin

Page 59    *Salmon Chief,* courtesy Vancouver Museum, photo by Kharen Hill

Reprinted with Permission:

Page 10    Aztec Warrior, *Eyewitness Aztec,* by Elizabeth Baquedano, published by Stoddart Publishing Co. Limited.,
Don Mills, Ontario

Page 20    Archaeopteryx illustration, *The Flying Dinosaurs,* by Phillip J. Currie, illustrations by Jan Sovak,
published by Red Deer College Press, ©1991

Page 22    Wind currents illustrations, *Natural History Series, Eagles,* by Aubrey Lang, illustrated by
Dorothy Siemens, published by Key Porter Books Ltd., Toronto, Ontario, ©1990

Page 28    Plains warrior's shield, Eyewitness North American Indian, by David Murdock, published by
Stoddart Publishing Co. Limited, Don Mills, Ontario

Page 30    Sky dance illustration, *Natural History Series, Eagles,* by Aubrey Lang, illustrated by
Dorothy Siemens, published by Key Porter Books Ltd., Toronto, Ontario, ©1990

Page 38    Bald eagle with egg, *Eyewitness Bird's Egg Handbook,* by Michael Walters, published by
Stoddart Publishing Co, Limited, Don Mills, Ontario

Page 42    Heilman's Proavis illustration, *The Manual of Ornithology,* by Noble S. Proctor and
Patrick J. Lynch, published by Yale University Press

Dinosaur-bird link chart, *Canadian Geographic,* illustrated by Jan Sovak

The Nature Conservancy of Canada is fortunate to have the support of many dedicated volunteers, who help us purchase and protect the best of our country's remaining natural habitats. We are particularly grateful to the following individuals for their support in conserving unique wildlife habitat in the Squamish/Brackendale region:

Peter Bentley, Vancouver

Mel Cooper, Victoria

Jack Munro, Vancouver

Michael Phelps, Vancouver

Fred R. Wright, Vancouver

W. Robert Wyman, West Vancouver

Without the contribution of these and many other prominent Canadians, The Conservancy could not have achieved its record of more than 1.2 million acres preserved for the benefit of future generations, nor pursue this important work in the future. We thank them and express our deepest appreciation for their services to Canada.

Robert S. Carswell
Chair, Board of Trustees

William B. Schwartz,
Past Chair, Board of Trustees

John H. Eisenhauer
Executive Director

Kirk R. Davis
British Columbia Director

The Nature Conservancy of Canada
2nd Floor – 827 West Pender Street
Vancouver, British Columbia, Canada V6C 3G8
(604) 684-1654
1-800-465-0029